The Hidden Girl

Return (Tapestry no.17 from Drawing no.41)

The Hidden Girl

The Journey of a Soul

MARIKA HENRIQUES

SHEPHEARD–WALWYN (PUBLISHERS) LTD

First published in 2018 by
Shepheard-Walwyn (Publishers) Ltd
107 Parkway House, Sheen Lane,
London SW14 8LS
www.shepheard-walwyn.co.uk

British Library Cataloguing in Publication Data
A catalogue record of this book
is available from the British Library

ISBN: 978 0 85683 522 3

Typeset by Alacrity, Chesterfield, Sandford, Somerset
Printed and bound in the United Kingdom
by Short Run Press

To children whom the world allows to suffer.

"I also speak to you as a witness.
 I speak to you, for I do not want my past to become your future."

ELIE WIESEL

Contents

Acknowledgements

My husband Wille for his patience, supportive listening and for giving me space and time to write. Teresa von Sommaruga Howard and Daphne Chappell for their meticulous editing and helpful comments. Kiersty Garbett for photographing the original images with painstaking and devoted care. My special thanks and deep gratitude to Roderick Peters for helping me to bring this book to birth with his continuous support, energy and time.

Foreword

In writing this book, my intention was to chart an inner journey rather than write an autobiography or a professional article.

I was shaped and my profession was determined by history. I was born in Budapest in 1935. During the Holocaust in 1944, separated from my family, I became a hidden child. I was nine years old. These dark times had a profound and lasting effect on me. That being a Jew was shameful and had to be hidden remained etched deeply into my being for decades.

Fascism was followed by communism. Persecuted once more, now for my middle class background, during the 1956 uprising at the age of twenty-one I escaped from Hungary. I crossed the border on foot amongst mine fields in minus 25 degrees Celsius. Eventually I arrived as a refugee in England.

In 1961 I married a Swedish Jew. In time I found my vocation and became a Jungian psychotherapist.

Occasionally I quote C.G. Jung, who was the founder of Analytical Psychology, best known for his archetypal theory and the collective unconscious. I refer to him at times, because his ideas were an integral part of the process of understanding myself and my images.

There were to be other major endings and beginnings in my life. The images, drawings, tapestries and poems, are woven together with my writing to tell my story. The story of wounding and healing. Myself and others.

To return to my tradition and to my people was a painstaking journey. It started with a major surgery and ended twenty years later on the pulpit, the bimah of a synagogue.

Introduction

The drawings and the tapestries in the book are not illustrations in the conventional sense. They came unexpectedly, from deep within me, to help me heal. Many came with poems. The text was written much later. It introduces the images, though it is not an explanatory text, but a story which concluded my healing and which I was only able to write two decades later. The narrative text can be read on its own without the images, which can be looked at separately.

I believe that to write a coherent narrative is very necessary, not only for Holocaust survivors, but also for anyone who has suffered trauma. It is a very important but a hugely difficult thing to do. I would like to show with my book that, nevertheless, it is possible.

For this reason, the drawings and tapestries are not interspersed in the narrative. They themselves constituted a process. First came the drawings, then the more consciously shaped tapestries, and only much later the story. This way of depicting and describing the healing process, the journey of the soul, also honours the time line.

It was difficult to decide whether to use a drawing or a tapestry because the drawings were frenzied feelings which needed fast expression. On the other hand the tapestries were slow in the making, they were a conscious working through those feelings with understanding and acceptance. The choice also depended on the context in which an image appeared, because the rawness of the drawings express better the depth of feeling which so unexpectedly surfaced from deep within.

However, all the images, the fifty-two drawings and the nineteen tapestries, appear as appendices at the end of the book.

1
The Operation

I was told one glorious Spring day that there was suspicion of cancer in me of a fast growing and lethal kind. I had to decide whether or not to have the major operation recommended by my consultant.

When I first heard the pronouncement of my medical adviser, I was shocked and shaken to the very roots of my being. I did not believe her. The whole situation resembled a bizarre if not mad dream. When slowly I began to comprehend the horrible reality of this medical statement there was one singular feeling which emerged with no uncertain clarity. An operation for me was unthinkable. I had to persuade the world around me of this indubitable fact and find alternatives for surgery.

I soon found out that the world and I were in fierce opposition. I could not take on board the medical view which warned me with increasing urgency of the risk I was taking. I unwaveringly stood my ground and opposed the operation. But my conviction that I did not have cancer was brushed aside as unworthy of serious attention.

For quite awhile I pitted my intuitive knowing against the medical world's accumulated and sensation-based expertise. It seemed vitally important to listen to my inner voice assuring me that there was no alien body invading my body. On the contrary it was the opposing outer opinion that felt like the invading and deadly force.

My mother's legacy lay heavily on me as well. It was her fateful belief that one goes to hospital once only and then only to die. She fulfilled her dark prophecy when at around my age she went to hospital for the first time and died after an operation for cancer.

I had never been to hospital. The very word 'operation' filled me with terror and was unimaginable. The anaesthetic held a particular dread. I, who liked to be in control, knew that this 'I' would have to be suspended now, would to all intents and and purposes in fact cease to exist and 'it' would be placed inert into unknown hands.

I could not submit to this.

But as the days and weeks passed, and disagreeable tests followed, doubts started to slip through the closed doors of my resolve. What if I was wrong after all? Suppose I did have the type of cancer predicted by the tests and scans and biopsies, and that I would die without surgery? I still had tasks to complete essential to the fulfilment of my life. I had not yet made my mark.

I was not ready to die.

The real battle now began in earnest. No longer fought between me and the outer world but within my inner world. And it raged over a dangerously long four months. The object fought over was survival. To have the operation or to go on refusing it. These choices were weighed with obsessional care in my mind's relentless scales to no avail.

Time became suspended. Nothing moved. The scales remained in balance.

In the outer world time passed regularly and it grew impatient with me. Both medical and family pressure intensified, pressurising me to accept that invasive surgery was the only option. I felt threatened and manipulated. The world viewed me as obdurate and irresponsible.

It was at this point, when the tension between me and the world became untenable, that something unexpected occurred which tipped the balance and unlocked the stalemate.

A myth entered my life rather abruptly with an unceremonious bang through my letterbox.

It was a Jungian sample journal from the USA. The article which caught my attention was called "Uncursing the Dark". It had a reference in it to the myth of Innana. I realised that this myth is described in *Descent to the Goddess* by Sylvia Brinton Perera.

In this Sumerian myth, Innana the Goddess of Heaven and Earth descends to the Underworld. There she is confronted by Innana's sister, Ereshkigal, ruler of the Great Below. It is a story of Descent, of Death and Rebirth, the encounter of Light with Dark. Reading it was a revelation and a recognition. I realised that I must, willingly consent to the operation. I had to learn that when Ereshkigal calls no one is exempt. She demanded that I submit to be cut open, that I trust her and her dark realm.

I felt I was at the start of a hero's, or rather a heroine's, journey. It meant that unlike the hero, who has to slay the dragon, I would have to lay myself in its sharp-toothed mouth, endure, and hope to come out shattered, with parts of my body torn away, but to emerge, like Innana, stronger, more complete. This required an active willingness to be open, to receive and to be operated upon.

About the same time that Innana appeared on my doorstep I also had a dream. An old woman appeared and said with gentle authority and great simplicity: "*Have the operation, you will feel better for it.*"

Both the dream and the appearance of the myth, so appropriate to my crisis, had an awesome effect.

I decided to obey the call of Ereshkigal and to follow the advice of the wise old woman. This was now my considered decision, born out of intense inner struggle and of synchronistic events rather than an acquiescence born out of fear and compliance.

I consented to surgery, and had the operation in the Autumn. I did lose vital parts of my body, but I did not die, and was told that I did not have cancer. (The Bed of Pain, see following page.)

It was uncanny, how at one level the operation repeated the wartime trauma of intrusion, terror, loss and grief. In both cases events were life threatening, unreasonable and abrupt. They were incomprehensible, beyond

The Bed of Pain (Drawing no.2)

The Bee

I saw a bee on the pavement,
amongst fallen leaves
and hurried footsteps.
Painfully, the honey-striped body dragged
along the black stone,
like an old memory dropped
callously out of mind.
Tender wings broken, lonesome it crawled
in the dust and the dark.
And my heart ached
as I wondered,
did it remember still,
the buzz and the whirl,
the sweet-smelling hive,
and the glorious flight
in never-ending
Summer-blue skies?

belief and beyond control. In both events the pain and suffering I had to endure were due to no lack or fault of mine. There was nothing so wrong in me then that I needed to be hidden or annihilated and there was nothing as diseased in me now that it needed to be cut out and destroyed although both times the authorities declared it so.

On the third day after the operation I felt very low. A few days later a close friend came to visit. She placed a box of crayons and a wad of paper on my bedside table and proposed that I drew how I felt. That was a strange suggestion. I could not draw. My hands behaved like a three year old's. I could only manage stick figures with large heads and no perspective. That same night however, I woke at 3.30 a.m. and began to draw.

Of all that was to follow in years to come this was perhaps the most significant moment of all. If I had not netted those fleeting thoughts and painful sensations, they would have dropped back into the unconscious and then nothing would have followed. But somehow I did.

It was as if the incision made in my body simultaneously also opened up parts of my psyche which were previously inaccessible to me. It made me realise that body and soul are one, and at the deepest level of the psyche they are indivisible.

Jung said "transformation is not just an airy fantasy but is a process that reaches down into the somatic sphere or even arises from it."

My process of becoming aware of my Holocaust experience began with the operation, through the body, allowing it literally to be cut open.

The images came unbidden at odd times and poured through me uncontrolled by conscious intent or design. They seemed strange and mostly incomprehensible outpourings. At the time of drawing I was unaware that they were unconscious expressions of my Holocaust experiences. I did not realise that the spirit within me was an energy, creating healing images to make order out of chaos. Nevertheless the act of drawing felt immensely healing.

First Steps (Drawing no.1)

It seemed as if my creativity, like bits of my body, were now rolling out of me, bumping along narrow hospital corridors, down the lifts, disappearing into the streets. I felt simultaneously empty, and in that hollow place in my middle, also full with a leaden heaviness. I feared that I would never be whole again. Yet this initial drawing indicated that despite the suffering and loss, the possibility of new beginnings was there as well.

2
The Drawings

"Bent to ceaseless labour
intent and earnest,
despite no promise
from the womb of Time
to grant completion,
I am hauling fragments
out of the Dark."

(*Marika Henriques*)

Depicting something is very ancient. Cave drawings from the Dordogne and elsewhere illustrate the fact that images were created long before written language was invented.

I wish to emphasise that images are multilayered, represent many things, have many meanings. I only focused on that level of the drawings which, in time, I realised depicted the Holocaust in order to recall and understand my Holocaust experience.

I made 52 drawings. 42 were made during four months, initially in hospital, then while convalescing. The last ten came over the next three years.

Jung believed, "that the unconscious goes straight for its goal which is to allow the individual to become whole". The drawings were the first steps on a long path of becoming more fully myself. They attempted to translate body memories into something more tangible to which I could relate and have a dialogue with. Intuitively I named the initial drawing First Steps. The potential, the promise of new life was always present, and like in physical labour hinted at a process which however difficult, will be in the end

The Flower

No seed, this strange flower, nestling softly
in rich soil, dreaming shyly of a golden sun.
This is a full bloom, reared in secret,
it's leaves hidden from hungry caterpillars,
it's petals sheltered from late frosts,
the centre a deep-red jewel, lighting up
a darkness in which it is embedded.
Shaped by time, it whispers of things to come.

Flowers (Drawing no.11)

Flowers (Drawing no.9)

Flowers (Drawing no.10)

The Orchid

I drove fast down
a leafy Irish lane.
Each day as sheep and
gorse beckoned,
I followed to pastures
just beyond.
But today into
my vision sprang
a grey stone wall,
and on it from a

mossy crevice, rose,
strangely, a single bloom.
I left the car and came
to have a closer look;
unmistakably purple-lipped,
there, like a soldier
on guard, erect,
stood an orchid.
And there too, stood I,
on the empty road

under slow-drifting clouds,
and for quite awhile,
there seemed to be only
the orchid and I.
And when I bade farewell
to moss and stone
and sky, I drove
on in peace, with
my thoughts in the flower,
and the flower in my heart.

endurable and worthwhile. (It was an amazing and with hindsight an amusing coincidence that when I arrived for my surgery I was mistakenly directed to the labour ward). A few days after my operation I was asked to get up and walk down the long hospital corridor. It was a brief but physically and emotionally painful journey. And yet as I dragged myself along, I thought of an astronaut landing on an unknown star (First Steps, see p.6).

There was a peculiarly uneven rhythm in producing the pictures. I had little control over how often or when I drew. My inner self urged, and I had to obey in spite of pain after surgery and exhaustion during recovery. During these weeks and months, I needed to continue going on being, feeling, dreaming, sensing and most of all drawing without impingement. Any disruption felt unendurable; a physically painful rupture.

Light and dark, death and rebirth are recurring themes in my drawings. Also the belief, that like in the Innana myth, there will be ascent after descent, that after suffering the dark night of the soul, light will be born out of abysmal darkness.

The negative elements often were unknowingly pictured together with the positive ones; for example Flowers (see facing page). Flowers represented the yearning for transformation, the growing from darkness to light. But the butterfly, symbol of the soul, (in ancient Greek butterfly and soul were the same word, psyche) had a more sinister significance for me. Children killed in the Holocaust scratched butterflies on the walls on their way to the gas chambers.

That a process of integration is long and arduous was not realised at the time of the drawings. I recall the alchemists' warning "that the operation fails many times, the retort can even explode... and the work must be started all over again..." I did not know then that part of my work was to retrace my steps moving in a circular spiralling way, over and over again, and that the process would take many years of painstaking and excruciating labour just as the alchemists had warned.

There were many premature jubilations, the sense that all is well, all is done. For example I actually believed that the triumphant picture Conquest (see p.10)

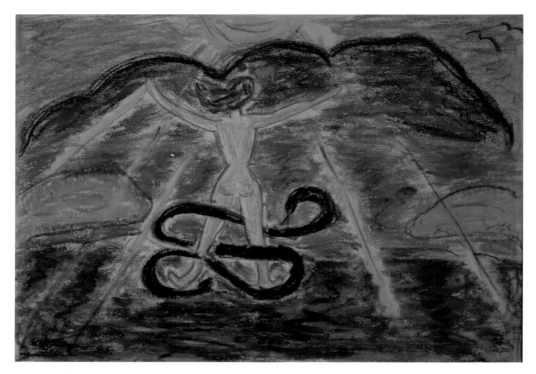

Conquest (Drawing no.19)

The Chaos Dragon (Drawing no.20)

was my last drawing. Yet a week later I had a nightmare. I don't remember the dream, only my pounding heart, my body slippery with perspiration as I woke trembling with terror. The next day I drew the terrifying Chaos Dragon (see facing page). I was not yet ready to heed psyche's teaching that after such blinding light, devastating darkness follows. From then on I was spiralling down into darkness and despair. The following drawings until Return (see p.ii)

were the result of this unremembered nightmare, attempting to image unbearable feelings. Yet that something new could emerge was poignantly imaged in the drawing The Jewel. This image is embedded in the text. This is because, by hindsight, I recognised that symbolically a precious treasure appears in it, which then runs through all the images, disappearing and reappearing not unlike the hero does in a fairytale. It foretells of value and hope, found and lost and found again, perhaps to be captured and held at the end of a long journey.

The Jewel (Drawing no.7)

Just as my unconscious struggled to come to light, so my conscious mind struggled to process its manifestations and tried to comprehend them. I began to seek out what I needed to know. Until I drew Return I had read about Jung but not Jung himself. I began to read his work avidly with a similar drivenness that produced the drawings. It made me realise that the mind-stunning experience of creating pictures happened because I was flooded with archetypal feelings and imageries.

I recorded my dreams, used the insights gained in my analysis and allowed my feelings to shape into poetry. Chance events, meetings, conversation with friends all aided the work of meaning-making. But what was essential was living with the images. I pasted them on my bedroom wall and took them on holiday. They were the first things I saw on awakening and the last before I went to sleep.

My drawings might seem chaotic and naïve but they are authentic expressions of my inner journeying, my progression from unconsciousness to more awareness of my Holocaust experience. They were never intended to be art.

3
Hiddenness

I went into "open hiding" when I was nine years old. This meant hiding as an Aryan under an assumed name. I was with strangers who kept me for money. They were janitors of a house my father had designed. They had two teenage children, a boy and a girl so there were five of us in their one room basement flat. There was a kitchen but no bathroom or toilet. I am not certain whether or not I was used or abused by these people. On the whole, events of these months of hiding slipped out of my mind like a pebble disappearing in a lake. I have reconstructions but few conscious memories of that time.

Oddly enough, my parents never asked me about my time in hiding. They were occupied with rebuilding our lives, and perhaps they thought it was easier for a child to forget if not questioned. The message seemed to be that I too must get on with my life. For decades I truly believed and maintained that nothing noteworthy had happened to me. I was living with some people in hiding and after the war I was reunited with my family. That was it. Nothing much to tell, was there?

That the Holocaust was a central issue in my life became apparent only in my analysis. At the time of the operation I had been in analysis for the past two years: Therapy (see following page). Until then, it remained hidden as I was in the Holocaust. I had blocked out, "forgotten" most events of that time. Did the waters of forgetfulness wash over the child, or did the adult deprive the child of memory? In the nights I tried to remember. My dreams hinted at my being presented as backward and hinted of evil men. I dreamt of a witch tearing apart a book entitled Hungary, scattering the pages so that it would not be possible to reassemble them. I dreamt that I lost my camera. I dreamt that I lost everything. I dreamt of madness and terrifying disintegration.

Therapy (Drawing no.4)

Daydream

in a vast sky
the orange moon
circles
motionless.
White deer graze
in the whispering
shadows the
garden sighs...
Silent wings
brush my face
lightly as I
dream
of weaving
bridges to the
laughing Sun.

I dreamt of pushing at a heavy door with all my might but when it opens my hands are only pushing into dense fog.

A dim awareness of something familiar started to stir in my mind. Something unthinkable, beyond reach, yet known...like in the dream where my hands were pushing through this light, impenetrable substance that reveals nothing...

Something which occurred a long time ago is here hurting me now... What have I suffered ...? By what violent or uncaring hands? I can almost feel it yet I cannot name it. Out of this ominous fog only a profound sense of pain and incomprehension appears.

How does this eerie sensing connect with the needless operation I have endured?

The awful anticipation... the resigned preparation... the dread... the syringe irrevocably removing from consciousness the bloody event... the hands which assaulted my body... whose hands... while I lay there inert and unprotesting... why did I let it happen... the gradual awakening of this nightmare unremembered... the sharp pain coursing through and through me...

Like a mysterious monster rising from the deep comes the tormenting question. How did this pain enter me? When? By what means?

The answer is hidden in the fog... And I am left wondering in the twilight space between knowing and not knowing...I endured for long the vague promise of twilight... I felt the dark touch of night... But dawn... will dawn ever break?

Once when in a therapy session I attempted to lie on the couch, as is customary in analysis, fell into deep terror, crouching, trying to hide. I stared at the white wall as if onto a screen. But the wall remained blank. No one keeps a secret as well as a child. Her survival depended on silence and I could not persuade the frightened nine year old in me to trust and speak out.

The Mute One (Drawing no.27)

My image, The Mute One (see facing page), expresses the horror of what it is like to be defenceless, without arms and without recourse to speech. Her eyes are enormous. What is she seeing? And why can't she tell? Oh, that dread, that terror is mute, unspeakable. It is the scream that cannot be screamed, the escaping feet pinned to the ground, the dry mouth, the body slippery with sweat, the hammering heart... I taped the drawing to the wall of my analyst's consulting room and on both sides of it I hung long streamers of miniature reproductions of Edvard Munch's painting "The Scream".

I felt guilty for not remembering. Does not the Torah repeat 169 times "zachor", "zachor" remember remember...There remained a stubborn hope in me that some day, in some way I might be able to cry out and bear witness.

There were many troubled feelings. Why did I survive and my cousin did not? Why did the world allow children to suffer and die? Why did my grand-mothers, my cousin, my aunt and uncle - why was my whole extended family killed?

The Chaos Dragon (Drawing no.20)

Of the many layers and levels of meaning this image depicts my particular experience of the Holocaust, the "Dark Times" – a time when the secure, known world shape-changed into a demented creature, a crazed monster pursuing its need to kill and destroy. It represented an evil force, all that is menacing, lurking in the dark, opposing order; it stands for terrifying chaos, releasing "unthinkable terrors".

4
Woundedness

It is unimaginable what people who survived the death camps, people who were hiding in terrible circumstances, had suffered. But I can only tell my story, tell of my woundedness. What I can offer for consideration to collective consciousness is that the wind of hate touched and traumatised everyone. Comparison is not useful. It is pointless.

When I returned to therapy after the operation and my analyst saw my drawing, The Chaos Dragon (see facing page), he said "there will be dark times ahead of us". It reminded me that my father had called 1944, when mad archetypal energies were loose in the world, "The Dark Times".

Bombing. It seemed interminable.

With photographic clarity I see my mother putting our heads in her lap, covering them with her old fur coat to muffle the sounds. When finally we emerged from the air-raid shelter we saw that our house had been hit. My home, my childhood home. Destroyed. Gone. We had to go and live in a ghetto, in one of the "starred houses" so called, because they displayed the Star of David, the discriminatory yellow star all Jews had to wear over the heart. As I write this, I hear Henry Dutilleux's piece of music "The Shadows of Time" (which he dedicated to the children of the Holocaust) where a voice stops the music by the question "why us, why the star?"

My mother's intuition saved our lives. One evening she said to our father "we are leaving". "But there is nowhere for us to go", countered my father. But she was adamant. We took off the yellow star from our clothes and left. Long we had to walk. No one, no friend or acquaintance would, or dared to take us in. My sister and I were eventually offered to stay the night by one

The Obliterated Child (Drawing no.23)

Who Told You

to recoil from pain
and admit to none
?

to rush and comply
to comfort and hold
to wave goodbye
without hesitation
to

hide your tear
and know no pain
to lie in the dark
and swallow your
fear.

The world is watchful
pretend you don't know it
put on your robe of
innocence the
smile

you have lost
that time so
long ago when
unprepared you
looked...

and into the face of
death

man-made and cruel
you were forced to stare
until you recoiled with
the shock

and buried the knowledge
the incomprehension
and locked it
away

with your scream
and the knife sharp
pain.

The key is turned
and thrown away.

Who told you

to recoil from pain
and admit to none
?

of our teachers. We stayed for two weeks. We had to sit in total silence. We knitted. And in the evenings, like Penelope in the Odyssey, we undid all the stitches in order to have wool available for the next day.

Then the hiding. On my own. I did not know where my sister or parents were or whether they were alive or not.

Only after the liberation in early 1945 did I learn that my mother and also my sister had been in open hiding. Before my father could arrange this for himself he was hiding for weeks in a bombed out house day and night. He was afraid of wild dogs, he told me. A brave Christian friend brought him food whenever he could. We also learnt that after we left, everyone in our "starred house" was killed – shot, and thrown into the river Danube.

During my time in hiding I was stripped of all that constitutes "I". My home, my family and friends, my possessions, my religion and especially my name. My past had to be wiped out and a new self had to be invented and adopted in order to save my life. Overnight I had to become someone else. Who was I? I lost my identity. Accordingly the drawing, The Obliterated Child (see facing page), which unexpectedly appeared decades later is defaced, scribbled over, crossed out.

Severed from everything safe and familiar I learned the meaning of fear, abandonment and the absolute necessity of hiddenness.

As in a shadowy dream a young German appeared with a round face and crinkly blond hair. In my mind he was billeted in the house where I was in open hiding. He became fond of me and often sought my company. When food became scarce (people cut off flesh from dead horses in the street) he gave me a blackbird he killed. He used to boast about participating in the killing of Jews on the shore of the Danube. Only my body holds the memory of the terror that must have engulfed me on such occasions. I cannot bear to imagine the effort required of my nine year old self to continue week after week to conceal her true identity in such dangerous company. And I have not gained accurate measure of the confusion this harrowing experience must have created in her heart and mind.

Survival (Drawing no.8)

Dying (Drawing no.33)

My drawing Survival (see facing page), was meant to be a happy picture celebrating the survival of my operation and the start of recovery. Dying (see facing page) simply attempted the opposite of the same scene, as it was born of a dark mood. Yet both feature a blood band representing the "Blue Danube" turned red with the blood of my people herded together, shot, and thrown into the river.

When I was speaking to a friend about the house where I was hidden I did not say hidden, I made a slip of the tongue and said the house in which I was buried. The association with burial is of course death.

I dreamt of a huge woman with a swastika pursuing two little girls. She threw one from a great height to her death, but the other one escaped and survived.

I understood that the dead child represented my destroyed childhood, the necessity to grow up overnight and the premature loss of innocence. Like many of the hidden children my surviving self became the silent carrier of a "terrible knowledge" (Jeffrey Jay).The knowledge of that unfathomable potential, that infinite capacity of brutality of man towards man. A knowledge which no one seeks, a burden no child should carry.

The terror which reigned outside, permeated my being insidiously and left an indelible mark. The fear I had felt during hiding attached itself after the war to ordinary everyday events and activities.

Though only few conscious memories remained of this time my body recorded, stored and remembered them. I suffered (and still suffer) from insomnia. Sudden inexplicable anxieties would surge through me at the least change in my daily life. Even minor separations could make me ill. In the nights, faceless terrors invaded my dreams, **Night Terrors** (see following page).

Because I had experienced at an early age what it was like not to have a safe place, I was forever looking for hiding places. Above all my priority was safety and that often meant retreat from life.

Night Terrors (Drawing no.22)

Night Terrors

Who are these ghosts?
The cobwebs they carry
where do they come from?
They suffocate, squeeze my heart,
turn my thoughts into icicles of terror.
They blur my vision with dusty bandages,
until I feel only, see only fear; a black
gaping hole, which widens, opens, widens, opens
like a terrible ravenous mouth.
Fear.
It turns innocuous objects, friendly gestures
inside out, until they become dark and threatening.
The horror of it.
Who are these ghosts?
Why do they come and
when will their visitations stop?
How can I, paralysed in their grip,
bid them go, fare they well?
They arrive at night, when dark is gathering

in faraway corners
and arrange themselves in tight
configuration around my bed.
They form an impenetrable circle.
It is always the same.
They do their job efficiently,
without rancour or malice.
They squeeze, they throttle, they blur.
They weave and wave and hold their fine net
under me, beyond me.
They leave only, when their work is done.
Dawn with impetuous fingers
opens my window wide
and pours in her sunlight.
I hold out both my hands
and bathe in the warmth
and cleanse myself in the light.
Gratitude.
Am saved once more.

For many years I worked as a qualified librarian. Amongst other library jobs I worked in the Folklore Society Library in UCL. Not many people visited it and I was the only staff. I felt content that I was as unsought as were the books. Echoes of my inner world, I immersed myself in the world of myths, fairytales and legends, cut off and undisturbed by a world which I conceived to be noisy, demanding and above all dangerous. I was hidden in a crypt, a burial place. I felt safe.

I believe that if one does not use one's unique talents they turn against one. And I was, until my analysis, in a profession unsuited to my particular gifts, which I believe contributed to my depressive episodes.

The Chaos Dragon (see p.18) depicts the terrifying underworld of the unconscious where my wartime memories lived and thrived and into which, like Innana who in the myth was going down into the 'Great Below', I had to descend. Descend into a force which opposes order, security and all that is familiar. The Spiral Snake (see following page) imaged my descent for a while into this place of chaos, the releaser of unthinkable terrors. Jung warned not to underestimate the danger of getting lost in chaos though it is also the *sine qua non* for renewal.

Mario Jacoby, a Jungian analyst, speaks eloquently of the chaos dragon as "representing fragmentation...the loss of the cohesive self, the threat to conscious control over unconscious forces..."

I think of depression not as a disorder but as distress, having to endure, as a defence against pain, a deadly emptiness, a kind of negative nirvana. A feeling that Nature had turned on itself, birthing only death and that Time was grinding on eternally unchanging. My few bouts of disabling depressions were always triggered by loss or some chaotic event in the outer world.

An instance. My father was ill, and I returned to Budapest for the first time fourteen years after the uprising in 1956. But when I arrived, where, in 1944, I and my people had to face a collective terror of physical death as well as mental disintegration, I did not survive the journey unscathed. My father died while I was in Budapest. The grief. I had to go and sign some documents in an office which was in the headquarters of the Hungarian Secret Police. I remembered it – with fear. People were tortured there. Having to go there,

The Spiral Snake (Drawing no.21)

The Chaos Dragon opened up into a blue-green Spiral Snake, and like a whirl-pool was sucking in the terrified figure. I was falling into a dangerous place, where archetypes dwell and childhood memories hide. The image indicated that I would have to re-live the suffering and divisions that my traumatic and prolonged experience had so insidiously deposited into my soul, like an evil cuckoo laying its alien egg to hatch. In time what emerged with unsuspected force was terror, deep mistrust, threat of disintegration and an all pervading hopelessness as well as helplessness.

the shock of return, compounded by my father's death made me very sick both in body and in spirit.

I was hounded by the terror of discovery ever since my time in hiding. After achievements or compliments I often felt like a fraud and feared that people would find out that I was impersonating someone who was not me.

For a long time I refused to look into The Well of Tears (see following page) fearful that I would drown. I knew I would find more and different losses. In 1956 at twenty-one I had to up and leave once more as there was again a threat to my secure existence. First Hitler, then Stalin. Again I had to leave my friends and family behind and this time also my country, tradition and language. At my first job in England my colleagues called me Mary. (Affectionately quoting every now and then Mary, Mary quite contrary). As a refugee once more I had lost my identity and had to recreate it.

So many losses. I had a recurring nightmare for years. I called it "the empty handbag" dream.

On discovering my gaping holdall had lost all its contents, my grief brought forth such animal sounds that people around me fled and I woke up in a state of uncontrollable sobbing.

In the story *Descent to the Goddess*, Enki, 'the God of Waters and Wisdom' fashioned two little mourners out of the dirt of his fingernails. They descended to the 'Great Below' and witnessed Innana's dark sister Ereshkigal's labour pains. Compassionately they echoed her every moan, followed her every move, bending with her pain like the wind. By recognising, understanding and accepting her suffering they met her deep need of mirroring, transforming not only her pain but her entire being. I realised from my nightmare how much my grief needed witnessing and brought The Two Little Mourners to life (see following page).

The Well of Tears (Drawing no.35)

The Two Little Mourners (Drawing no.26)

5
Alongside Drawing

But life was not only suffering the past, it was also living life in the now. Alongside drawing I also finished my training as a psychotherapist and built a full practice. I brought to this work my whole being and all that nurtured it. Books and lectures but also music, poetry, walking in the woods and watching the waxing and waning of the moon. I work long term, mostly with people who sustained early damage in their lives. Jung's idea of the "the wounded healer" expresses why I believed that I would be of help to others. I became deeply engaged in helping people who were not allowed to speak, or could not express their feelings. I endeavoured to facilitate their giving voice to their Mute One (see following page), to allow their repressed feelings to emerge. I found that my wounding has created a space within me which could hold and contain the pain of my patients.

It is extraordinary to have learned what a large proportion of the hidden children in later life chose to go into the helping professions: medicine, social work, and above all therapy. The articles in a Newsletter called the "Hidden Child" were written by a psychiatrist, an analyst, a psychologist and a psychotherapist.

Despite my fear of madness and disintegration, as part of my training, I volunteered to work for about half a year in a hospital on the psychiatric ward. Though at first I had the urge to leave I persisted and stayed on. I worked one to one with a drug-disturbed young man, attended all meetings and followed the ward rounds. I even achieved a moderate success influencing a system which was functioning benevolently, yet was not fully aware of its own power.

I also decided to return to Hungary for a visit but this was a fraught decision.

The Mute One (Tapestry no.2)

My Autistic Child

Under secret cover
like crustacean shells
they lie;
these precious, hidden,
gossamer feelings
unformed,
unthought,
never-daylight seen...
like light foam skimming
the stormy,
night engulfed winter-seas,
unfathomed,
non-worded,
hardly happenings
...how can
you tell...
with what untried sounds
could you entrust the world
of lidless eyes and
careless, noisy ears
these secret-shy
jewels
shining faintly
In the mute bowels
of your being?

I was invited to attend a conference in Budapest but soon after I had filled in the required application form I had a dream.

> *I was at an airport, getting ready to board a plane. There was a flurry of activity, I had difficulty in getting all my things together and I had mislaid my handbag. When at last I had found it, I saw with dismay that my passport was missing. The plane took off without me.*

I realised that not only was I emotionally unprepared to go, but returning to my home town under the aegis of a conference was inappropriate. I had to go and face what I was afraid to meet and go for no other reason. I had to wait for another year before I felt that I was ready to go. I then did return to Budapest but I could not set foot in it. I could only view the city from a hired car for the entire period of my stay. Portrait of my Analyst (see following page) pictures the need to hide safely in his mind while I was away and evoked old fears and needs.

I began to write and to publish. Nine months after drawing The Heart Flower (see following page) I published a paper on the "Transcendent Function" in the Jungian journal Harvest. Other professional publications followed. A week after I made the Snake Girl (see p.33) The C.G. Jung Analytical Psychology Club – London invited me to give a seminar on the Innana myth. I was delighted. It was pleasingly synchronous to have been given the opportunity to talk about this particular myth which so powerfully intervened in my life. In time I have given talks to other professional organisations including one of my training bodies, The Guild of Psychotherapists.

Yet I was still hiding (The Forest (see p.34)). I learned it well. No one realised it. Which was after all the essence of the exercise.

Portrait of my Analyst (Drawing no.44)

The Heart Flower (Drawing no.42)

The Snake Girl (Drawing no.47)

Dawn

Like a child in play,
the Earth lies breathless;
branches of the birch
cradle for the moon
unwilling to end her journey.
Anticipation like birds
in their nests
stirring,
waiting,
for the surprise
of the day.
The eyes of the lake
still
blind
with the night...
dawn arises from shadowy dreams.

The Forest (Tapestry no.6)

Bubble

Light is giving birth to darkness,
the bird swoops upon its prey.
Fear like bindweed
creeps into the centre,
leaf and petal
falls and fades.

But in her bubble
undisturbed
the small child plays.

6
Yad Vashem and the Healing Nightmare

Few months after I began to write about the drawings I attended a conference in Jerusalem, entitled "The Hidden Child". There I met hundreds of
the "others". During this profoundly moving gathering the decades of silence
was broken. We shared stories, tears and addresses, and felt the solace
of belonging, as if we were part of a lost and reunited family.

While in Jerusalem, I visited Yad Vashem, the Memorial to people killed in
the Holocaust. The Children's Memorial's solemn interior is lit by only one
candle but it is reflected through the glass structure a thousand times.
A recorded voice recited the name and age of each child murdered in the
Holocaust. It was early morning and I was the only one there. And as I
listened to that endless and hollow litany, as the names of one million
murdered children echoed, one by one through the empty hall, I gradually
collapsed under their weight. Huddled by the flame of that one flickering
candle, unseen and unheard, I finally wept. I wept for myself and for each
of the others. The dead ones. In those infinitely sad, slow-moving moments
I began to reconnect with my heritage, my untended Jewish roots.

For many months after my visit to Jerusalem, I was occupied with the
question of evil. What is it? Where does it originate? How can it grip and fill
the human heart so utterly, that all its humanness is lost? Is it in all and
everyone? What does it take for the crouching beast to flex its muscles
and pounce? I watched every programme on television on the Holocaust and
its anniversary, also other genocides and other atrocities. I listened and
I watched. I heard the accounts of tortured victims all over the world, from
Bosnia, India, South Africa, from Thailand, Tibet, South America... Articles,

books and even people came my way unsolicited, as I was driven by my relentless questioning. I did not know what I was searching for but I had to go on with my quest all the same. I immersed myself into a nightmare world by day and by night, I could not stop.

A few months after I visited Jerusalem I had my worst Holocaust nightmare.

The nightmare.

I stand on the sixth floor of a block of flats intending to take the lift down. Suddenly it becomes utterly dark, there is only black-ness. A blackness not found in nature. I can't believe that this is happening. It is horrendous. Then on a wall behind me, a pro-jection appears, and in it, framed like a picture there is a face, fluid, evil, ever-changing, a face which is human, yet non-human. It all happens in a micro-second, but the dread is unbearable.

(I actually live on the 6th floor of a block of flats.)

Although I woke up in terror, I somehow managed to forget the dream. Like my time in hiding, the dream too, dropped out of my mind. But the images, the blackness and the evil face returned in time to haunt me. Like Night Terrors (see p.24), they held me in their paralysing grip, so that I could not think or feel my way around them.

Six months later, Dr. Harry Wilmer, a Jungian analyst from America came to London and I went to hear him talk. The title of his lecture was a quote from Longfellow, "A heart for any fate". I had heard him talk before and was deeply moved by his work with Vietnam veterans. The Healing Nightmare in my title comes from Harry Wilmer's article "The Healing Nightmare: the study of the war dreams of Vietnam combat veterans". He occupied the place of "wise old man" in my heart. The patient he talked about this time had a dream in which the supernatural appeared similarly to mine in a curiously bounded way. A deep longing surfaced in me as I listened. I wished that Harry Wilmer would attend to my dream. At the end of this talk he unexpectedly announced, that there was time for some dream-work. Anyone who wanted a dream looked at was invited to put their name in a hat.

I knew that this was providential, that my dream had to be the one chosen. I had no doubt at all, that something so profoundly significant in my inner world as this dream, would be met in the outer one. A medley of emotion surged through me, as indeed it was my name which was pulled out of the hat. I was tearful with excitement, gratitude and anticipation. Like many times before, the mysterious coincidence which Jung called synchronicity made me feel as though I was held and helped by a power beyond my control and comprehension.

I believe that an injury one receives from the collective, can only be healed by the collective. It felt right and natural, that reticent as I am by nature, I was now standing in front of a large group, recounting my dream, revealing the petrified terror hidden within me. The focused and serious attention I received from this group for almost an hour, gave weight to my dream, validated my experience of hiding and gave it the significance I myself could not grant. Because the group acknowledged the deep wounds caused by "The Dark Times", they could now slowly begin to heal.

As Harry Wilmer guided me gently through the dream, I realised that it had a definite purpose. I knew already that I was searching for something since my journey to Jerusalem. The nightmare now revealed the meaning of my quest.

With Harry Wilmer's help I understood that the dreadful blackness in the dream signified the diffused and amorphous awareness of the "terrible knowledge" of a terrible world which I had carried within me since I was nine years old. But the dream did not end with the blackness. I had to remain up there on the sixth floor and wait until the terrible apparition emerged from this unfathomable darkness. I was then compelled to look for a fraction of a second into the formless, ungraspable face of Cosmic Evil.

I felt as if I had travelled through the Infinite, where my parallel worlds, "I know", and "I don't believe it", could meet and re-arrange themselves. I was now able to say, as Jung did, when asked about God, I don't believe, I know. I know that Absolute Evil exists.

I understood that once I had accepted the reality of Evil, I would have to let go of it. I do not mean that I had to forget what I saw. I mean that it is neither possible nor wise for me to probe into the mystery, the nature and origin of Darkness. To have been touched by it, to have seen it for an everlasting second is enough. I have to let go of the nightmare, take the lift down to the ground, go out into life, and while remembering the past and trusting the future, live fully in the present, the "hic et nunc", as Harry Wilmer called it. I understood that was the message of my nightmare and also the answer to my quest.

I was no longer desperate to go on searching in the fog for my lost memories. I knew enough already. I knew that part of my story included hunger, cold and abandonment, that I lived a life of fear, day by day, heart-beat by heartbeat, with incomprehension and unspeakable loneliness as constant companions during times of terror and upheaval.

It took time to realise that what mattered more than lost memories was that I encountered a world steeped in hideous darkness when I was such a young child. And the belief I held ever since, that what I have experienced could happen again, anywhere at any time. There could be no mix and match in my psychic paintbox. The trust that the world could also be ordinary and fairly predictable was destroyed for decades. That was the real wounding.

I looked up the stanza in Longfellow's poem, "The Reaper and the Flowers" from which Harry Wilmer took the title of his talk. It read:

> "Let us, then, be up and doing,
> With a heart for any fate
> Still achieving, still pursuing,
> Learn to labour and to wait."

7
The Last Drawing and Writing

After what seemed a long and harrowing time, I surfaced from the unconscious, from the belly of the Spiral Snake (see p.26), from the darkness and madness of confronting my Holocaust experience. In the myth Innana, at one point in her journey, is suspended from a peg in the 'Great Below' while her  dark sister Ereshkigal lies moaning giving birth. In the story the source of torment is also the spring of new life.

I sensed that I was unutterably altered by my descent to the the 'Great Below'; that having survived the ordeal new tides were gathering. I knew that my drawing Return (see p.ii) was a significant picture. But at the time I thought it only meant that my return from the belly of the Spiral Snake brought more con-  sciousness and more meaning. As with some dreams, it took years to understand its full meaning. But I felt better.

I allowed other feelings beside grief to surface. I had less pain in my body. I wrote more poetry, published more and felt lighter. As my terror of the world decreased somewhat, I began to find my fighting spirit and was able to voice controversial or unpopular ideas: The Egg (see following page). I had more fun and creative fulfilment. In terms of outer events, I became more active and influential in my professional life. It was also at this time that I was working on a psychiatric ward.

The Egg (Drawing no.34)

The Egg

There was a me
that no one knew,
in a marvellous silvery egg
it grew.
Oh, it was cherished
and how it was praised,
for the pleasure it gave
and it's exquisite hue.
(Kept of course safe from
where the North wind blew.)
But when on a fine
Summer day it finally hatched,
well then, out of this
wonderful egg, with a
whirl and a whistle
a small monster flew,
the me that no one knew.

Death (see following page) was my last drawing, portraying a dream.

> *I am in a school. Our task is to draw Death. This is to be our last drawing. I have an image of a huge dark spider but reject it. Then I see a beautiful gnarled old tree with a sun in its huge branches. It reminds me of Van Gogh's painting the "Sower". There is also a half-open door. I feel that I need more time. I have no paper to draw on. I am offered paper and some coloured pens. I am still selecting the right piece of paper when I wake up...*

I have always feared death. And since life and death are inextricably linked, I could just as well say that I have feared life.

My parents perceived me as a sensitive and imaginative child, a "schöngeist" and overprotected me even before 1944. I was never taken to a cemetery. I recall that I was not allowed to see the film "Bluebird", because it had a scene with the dead grandparents.

It was in stark contrast to my sheltered upbringing that I had discovered death. Once when in hiding I came out of the air-raid shelter, unaccompanied as usual, I saw people carrying what seemed to be two large pieces of wood. But I felt that there was something strange about them. I went to have a closer look and saw that the pieces of wood had hair blowing in the wind. These were no tree trunks. This was Death walking past. I was singularly unprepared for this scene and I believe that it contributed to my experience of the world as an incomprehensible and frightening place from which I continued to hide for years to come.

The dream-maker portrayed not a grim reaper but a sower, a winter tree, a setting sun and a door ajar. The tree would carry blossoms again in the Spring, the setting sun would rise again next morning and the door was opening as well as closing. In beautiful symbols the dream showed the cycles of death and rebirth. That "waxing and waning make one continuous move." Life is a process, Jung wrote, "and the end of every process is its goal and life ends in death."

Death (Drawing no.52)

Quiescence

How long since I sat
under my Summer tree,
my heart full of
blossom and bird song?
The sun, a pale prayer
In the stiff arms of
my Winter tree lies,
no sounds now,
the day shivers,
the door is ajar.

My dream, Jung and the poet D.H. Lawrence said the same thing:

> *"Oh build your ship of death, oh build it in time,*
> *And build it lovingly and put it between the hands of your soul."*

I carry these words and the dream images in my heart like fearless banners throughout the rest of my life's journey.

With my last drawing, Death (see facing page) the drawings ended. There were now fifty-two pictures like in a deck of cards, like weeks in a year. There was a sense of completeness about them. I felt something had been rescued from the dark, that like scintillae the drawings brought forth some light from the depth illuminating my experience of the Holocaust.

Gradually, after the drawings ended I began to write about the images. I veered between the intense emotions which gave birth to the drawings and the detached thinking necessary to give them meaning. Though the writing is raw, full of unprocessed painful feelings, one continuous scream if you like, or else hiding behind copious quoting of Jung and other theoreticians, I still value the book as a brave attempt to make sense of the drawings, to create some order out of what often felt to be bewildering chaos.

Jung talks of the timeless quality of the unconscious which has also an accurate time where "everything already happened and yet is unhappened, is already dead yet undead." During writing I discovered the astonishing correspondence between the dates of my wartime experiences and the date of drawing most of my pictures. The most striking one was that I went into hiding on the 17th October 1944 and on the same date 45 years later I made my first drawing. The significance of this date was not known to me at the time.

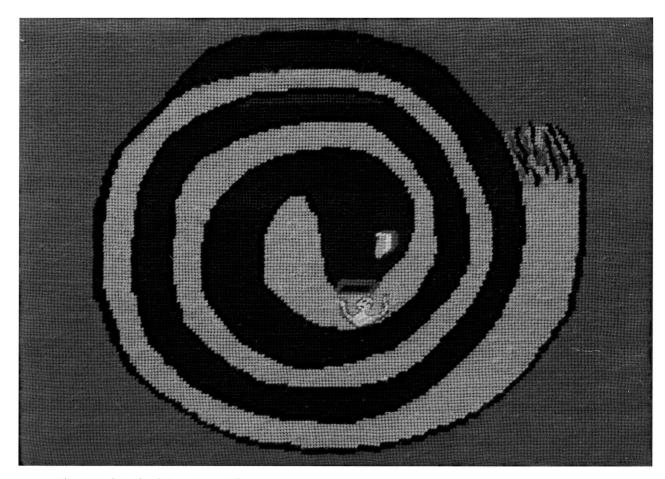

The Spiral Snake (Tapestry no.3)

One has to endure the descent, the dark night of the soul more than once. As in a spiral, one descends deeper each time, and each time one returns higher, one evolves, transforms further. But completion can only be aimed at, it is not ever granted.

8
The Rift

Though I returned from the 'Great Below', from the Spiral Snake's belly (see facing page) with more meaning, and understanding of my nightmare, it did not complete my inner journey as I yet again thought.

Two years later and the Holocaust cast its monstrous shadow over the analytic space. A number of the later drawings portray tense and stormy sessions during which the analytic vessel started to shake, as illustrated by the Four Sisters, Defeat, and Arrows drawings (see pp.46–7). My analyst and I endured them but we did not discuss or look at them too deeply. That is why I think that the Spiral Snake had not given up its wounding intent, why it spewed out its dark venom so unexpectedly.

The Dark Times of 1944 reappeared in the consulting room, and in the ensuing months I re-lived with my analyst the repressed and terrifying time of my wartime experience. To be compelled to face my traumatic injuries in the immediacy of the analytic space meant chaotic confusion and almost unbearable pain.

Unconscious forces pushed and pulled us about, relentlessly tossing us into a vicious archetypal pas de deux in which it was impossible to know who was who and what was what. Trust was replaced by betrayal and we began to experience each other as destructive combatants rather than the uniquely reciprocal companions we were. Was it that sadistic elements were pulled forth from my analyst, or was it my deeply sub-merged victim self that controlled and manipulated the dance in which my analyst was compelled to become the contemptuous and merciless Nazi tormentor? (The Sky Father, see p.48.)

The Four Sisters (Drawing no.31)

Defeat (Drawing no.32)

Arrows (Drawing no.40)

These were truly terrible times and as the wind of hatred blew through us it succeeded in breaking up the analytic temenos. Some people I had turned to suggested that I should, even that I must leave my analyst. But instinctively I knew that not only would that be wrong but that it would be injurious because if I left, the wartime trauma would remain fixed, unchanged. Intuitively I knew that I had to return, that only then could there be a possibility for the past to be transformed.

Longfellow's words "*to labour and to wait*" were never more essential.

Though I suffered terrible pain, disorientation and despair during the weeks I stayed away from my analyst, I did return. As I intuited, this traumatic disruption eventually brought priceless and transforming gifts.

It took time, a long time, but healing began when internally I formed my own meaningful explanation of what had happened. It was our identification with huge compelling archetypal energies which clouded our reason and dimmed

The Sky Father (Tapestry no.13)

Jung writes "that in such terrible times it is only the analyst's knowledge which remains the one dim light in the darkness." I felt that even this faint light was extinguished at times; indeed it seemed that all light had gone, all goodness had drained away, that there was only darkness and madness aboard. We turned into warring enemies.

our eyes to the truth. I realised that the passive and suffering victim and the active and aggressive victimiser were two aspects of the archetype of abuse and I understood that it was split between us. I realised that both of us were both victim and victimiser and that we injured each other.

I now could begin to differentiate between the personal and the universal, so vitally important because it strengthens consciousness. I experienced huge relief that on the personal level our dedication to the quest for truth and our trust in each other was not permanently damaged.

There were other gifts, other discoveries as well.

So important for Holocaust survivors and such a huge achievement, I could now slowly also begin to differentiate between the now and the then, between present and past.

The world also started tentatively to appear different. I saw that its space was enormous and held everything. Famine and war, cruelty and persecution as well as beauty and goodness. Stars and spring flowers, creepy crawlies but also water lilies.

I could now bear witness not only to Evil but also to Goodness, to the islands of light, the scintillae in the sea of darkness. My rescuers kept me for money, but there were others who for no gain whatever, risked their lives to save children. There were, and are and always will be a handful of remarkable people whose exceptional courage and humaneness are beacons, shining like the single candle in the Children's Hall in Yad Vashem, and are reflected a thousand times.

I looked at all my drawings portraying a snake and realised the huge power of the snake symbol containing both death dealing and life enhancing forces. The Spiral Snake (see p.44) was not wholly negative, it did not intend to kill. But it demanded a sacrifice. If I were to start to haul myself out of the Holocaust I had to sacrifice, give up the familiar notion of being and living as a hidden victim prescribed for me by the Nazis. And even more agonisingly to realise that darkness and aggression is also part of myself.

These dark and terrible times in my analysis were the nearest to my experiencing my wartime trauma. It had to happen just as the dreaded operation had to happen. It felt like a tectonic shift. It was necessary to re-enact the wounding so that not only the Chaos Dragon (see p.18) but I too could have control, differentiation; could make order and meaning of my wartime experience. And become conscious of it so hopefully I would not need to repeat it again.

That we both survived these dangerous and destructive times was a triumph and credit to us both. The frightful waves which tossed us about subsided and were gone, while we remained enclosed in the once more calm and safe analytic space. We continued, stronger and perhaps a little wiser, our work on my recovery, on the transformation of mere survival to full autonomous living for a few more years to come.

9
Tapestries

*"She put the thimble on her knotted finger with the solemnity
of a priestess performing a rite."*

*"Embroidery is more natural than oil painting, the swallows
are embroidering the sky for thousands of centuries."*

The idea of making tapestries came to me unexpectedly during a concert of
a late Shostakovich symphony.

As I listened to the music I noted how the secondary themes threaded in and
out of the main theme, weaving a unity of wholeness. Threads, weaving,
sewing, stitching. I realised that images need to remain visual, that they, like
dreams, are their own interpretation. I decided to return to the drawings and
make tapestries of some of them. Intuitively I knew that I would have to
thread things together. But it was a strange insight. Just as I could not draw,
I could not easily sew either. But by now I trusted that just as when I needed
to draw I would be able to overcome my ineptitude. I did not want to learn
how to make tapestries, I wanted to make them in order to learn from them.
I realise that my craftsmanship is untutored, but I feel that this is somehow
right, better suited to these archaic images.

Louise Bourgeois says:

*"All women in my home used the needle, the magic power of the needle.
The needle is used to repair damage...it is never aggressive. It's not a pin."*

Embroidery is traditionally a feminine activity, something women have
practiced since antiquity to express their thoughts and feelings and also

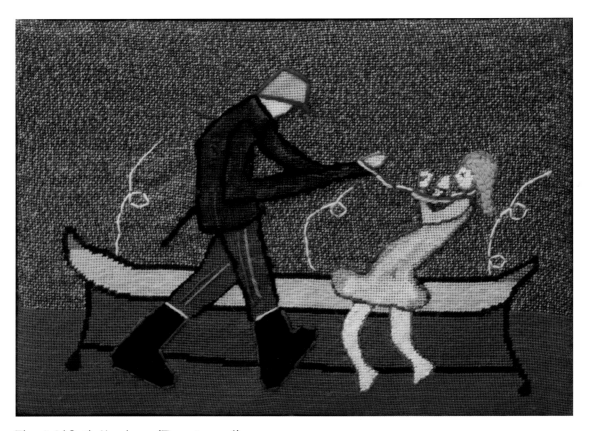

The Acid Bath Murderer (Tapestry no.1)

This picture is linked with The Chaos Dragon. With only slight variations, and always with the intent to kill, this image often appeared in my dreams. And I always escaped, but only just, in the last desperate second. The rest of the dream-time was filled with terror. The ABM's particular method of killing was a complete disintegration of being. After its visitation the soul was rendered sterile, a wasteland of hopelessness.

their experiences which they could not have voiced otherwise. Waiting, industry, perseverance and patience are all part of needlework.

Like many women before me I also wanted to make use of the power, the magic of the needle to repair damage. In contrast to the knitting in hiding, the stitching of the tapestries would not be unraveled, they were to serve meaning not futility. They were making things permanent.

Perhaps the only way to assist health and wholeness is by working through fragments. Behind the making of the tapestries was my desire to stitch my wartime experiences together to make the many fragments into one. The making of the tapestries was the continuation and, as I thought, the last one in my process of becoming aware of my experiences of 1944. I had been drawing for three years, I had been writing for three years and I was to stitch for three years. The whole process took about ten years. The drawings served as sketches from which I developed seventeen tapestries. With the drawings my repressed feelings found expression, with the book I made meaning of them, with the making of the tapestries I gave substance to the images. Stitching was also to do with acceptance. I was profoundly engaged in the making of them. But while drawing was relatively fast, with the tapestries I had to stay with one image, one anguished feeling week after week, often months after months there was no escape, no avoidance. And I had to repeat this seventeen times. Working through the fragments was painstaking and painful.

A good example is the Acid Bath Murderer (see facing page), ABM for short. He appeared in a dream as a Nazi and is the most direct image of my Holocaust experience. In the drawing he has a swastika on his helmet (see p.104). But unlike the Nazi death dealing swastika, unconsciously I drew it the opposite way, signifying life, much like the ancient sun wheel. The ABM's huge black boots and the swastika were the only discernible remains of my nine year old's war time experience. Whether the image was a true recollection or a fantasy I could not then tell for certain. But I did not demand from my nine year old self more proof to substantiate her story, and I did not doubt my unconscious which created the image.

The Dancer (Tapestry no.9)

The Dancer

Sun and Moon my tambourine
the boundless sky my cloak.
From the earth with mindful eyes,
an ancient serpent slowly stirs.
My feet between the serpent's coils,
in spinning darkness, soaring light,
I am the joyful, the triumphant,
I am the Spirit of the dance.

Every morning and every night I looked at the drawings pasted on my bedroom wall and conversed with them. But I only managed to steal furtive glances at the ABM's frightful countenance, and his featureless face never once looked back at me. With him I could not have a dialogue.

But when six years after the drawing, now framed as a tapestry, and once again hung on my bedroom wall, I found that I liked it. It was a good tapestry. I became more aware that in the dream it was I who survived and the ABM who died in the end. As I assimilated the message of the ABM it had lost its power and I could start conversing and have a relationship with it.

Each time I began a tapestry, there was a feverish need to to see the image emerge, and towards the end a reluctance to finish it. The tapestries urged me along often ruthlessly, because they needed to appear and demanded to be seen. Yet every time I cut the thread I could say goodbye to much of the pain and the past did not lie so heavily on me.

There was also a positive aspect, a positive charge in stitching. I am an intuitive person and not very good with what I think of as "real things". But now everything in the realm of sensation became exciting. I started to see where previously I only looked. I became interested in how things were made and as I stitched I became aware of the amazing shape of the human body. It was more than pleasurable to hold a ball of soft wool in my hands, more than satisfying to listen to the soothing sound the thread made as I pushed the needle in and out of the canvas. I was utterly engrossed in the work and also utterly enchanted. On the other hand I practically had to stop my main relaxation, music and reading, in order to have enough time and energy for stitching. I had no choice, I simply could not concentrate on anything else.

Slowly, stitch by stitch, the tapestries came into to existence, one by one. I gave them life, and in turn they gave me life also. I had more of myself, I became a different person. I learned that a bit of disorder was not necessarily a disaster. I gave more room to the non-rational side of things, I struggled less, and risked more. I have learned less control and more abandon. I definitely laughed more.

Forsaken (Tapestry no.10)

Lodestar

Cast into the attic
like a broken toy, forgotten,
unknown even to herself,
she huddles in a corner
dressed in dusty shadows
and seems to be waiting.

Needy, she knows no hunger,
wounded, she feels no pain,
she is a pauper full of riches,
she is the child in my dreams.

I long to touch her, feed her,
brush her tangled hair.
If I could weep her tears
and laugh her frozen laughter,
a lodestar she would sparkle
and give direction to my heart.

Lullaby

it is for you
the poplar plays
a tune
with the visiting
wind, and the
old church a
song of
evening bells.
The jasmine offers her scent
and the forest
a basket of berries.
I shall steal
pink ribbons
from the departing sun,
and together
we will spy on the
young moon
as she tries on her
silver crown.

It occurred to me that I could have called the Dancer (see p.54), dancing from the coils of the snake, "Recovery", because the word in Hungarian is closely linked to the word "snake".

Change can sometimes be sudden and swift or it can be imperceptibly slow. Like my tapestries where each final image appeared (I counted once) through twenty-four thousand small stitches, similarly my becoming more fully myself came about with small, hardly discernible movements. In my case change took time. Two decades.

Only after I finished making the tapestries did I fully appreciate the dream I had before the operation ten years before, in which the old woman urged me to have the operation, to allow myself to be laid open, to endure and to accept. "*You will feel better for it*" she had said. How infinitely wise she was.

All was done through image. It made me realise that healing lay in the imagination itself. As Jung had said "concepts are coined and negotiable values, images are life."

The entire experience from drawing and writing to stitching was immensely healing and transformative. The effects of hiding no longer ruled my life utterly.

The Torah instructs: "*only guard your soul carefully, lest you forget what your eyes saw.*"

I felt that with the tapestries my images were now complete. My uncommunicable memories were now shown and thus became silent but active witnesses. I no longer felt guilty. When I finished stitching I felt that I had fulfilled a sacred responsibility.

I had a talk and an exhibition of the tapestries, called "every stitch a tiny step", at the Royal Overseas League, Piccadilly under the aegis of The C.G. Jung Analytical Psychology Club London. As I prepared for the exhibition I struggled with an almost unbearable tension which I believe to be the unbidden legacy of all hidden children of the Holocaust. The tension between needing to be hidden and the longing to emerge. I had to fight mightily with a demonic/angelic figure which Donald Kalsched, a Jungian analyst talks about; one which wanted to protect me from being seen and therefore harmed, but one which also stopped me developing and changing and going forward in my life. It took me a whole year before I agreed to the request of the Jung Club. When the question arose how to present the tapestries it became essential to convey my experience of the many being one. I decided to present them as a collage where the images were attached to each other, yet where each had its own space. The order in which the tapestries were exhibited were different to the order in which they were created and I was surprised and pleased that the images fell into order in a swift, natural way. The image for example of the hidden child, Forsaken, (see p.56) found its space intuitively in the centre.

I was moved by a comment from the audience that the collage looked like a butterfly, meaning also psyche, soul, in ancient Greek. I was glad that I did not remain hidden, glad that I had the courage to stand up, glad to experience that instead of being harmed I was seen and appreciated. Encouraged to live the life of soul.

It seems that the experience of hiding leads to a need to return. I returned to Budapest for the third time, well into the first year of making the

Collage of Tapestries for the exhibition

tapestries. This time I found the house where I was hidden, not only through painstaking research but also through a series of amazingly synchronistic events. Though finding and being in the place of my hiding was painful, it had also an instantaneously liberating effect. It was as if the fragmented past of 1944 came together. I found that the half memories and fearful fantasies were actual remnants of real occurrences. I met an old lady in her nineties living in the house, who said that she knew, although she had never really seen me, that I lived with the janitors. She also told me that indeed there was a German soldier billeted in the house. He was in love with the janitor's daughter.

I realised through Night Terrors (see p.24) which placed itself opposite to Return (see p.ii) in the exhibition, that I made fifty-two drawings and that it took me fifty-two years to find the house which sheltered me from death. The feeling of terror, which, like a bad spirit persecuted me for decades, now found a containment and a resting place in the house. All was now located in it and I could come and go freely at last. I began to walk, take the tram, the metro and began to rediscover and remember the city. No longer dispossessed I repossessed it.

I returned to Budapest the fourth time a year later. Finally I was able to take my niece, born in England with me. She had asked for this journey for years. To be a guide to someone else made Budapest truly my own again. I showed it off proudly to my niece and hoped that in time it would connect her to her roots and add something to her identity. It was as if the ghostly mist which covered the city for decades had lifted, and I saw how beautiful it was. To discover that the war, the Nazis, did not succeed in robbing me of my city, my birth town where I lived my first twenty-one years was a triumph. It was a great joy to recollect that its smells, its flowers, its history and culture shaped me and my destiny.

I began to stitch the ABM before this journey and completed it after my return. On the plane on the outward journey I read in the magazine provided that the last Russian troops left Hungary that very month.

Bird and Snake (Drawing no.43)

The Kingfisher

a flash of blue
a splash in the green,
an arrow from the
skies to the edge
of deep water darts.

... kingfisher
blazing jewel,
lit by a thousand suns...

From the dark depth
a dream is caught,
a swift delight is
beheld for a moment
then flown and gone.

When back in London I had a dream, in which the floor of the kitchen, the central place in my home, had been cleaned up of the shit which covered it, and I was allowed to have a glimpse of an emerging pattern; something new and beneficial I felt when awakening: Bird and Snake (see facing page). But an indication also that my inner journey was not over yet. I had to "labour and wait" still.

The One-Eyed Stone (Tapestry no.7)

The Diver

"Follow your dreams" he said.

Fins and bones the
colour of amber, he
gave me his treasure,
this fish that stirred
like new life
In a womb, down
In the ancient bed
of the ocean.

"Follow your dreams", he said.

the cat to share
her awesome secret
came, huge hunger
hissing from her bony
mottled frame. Fierce
she jumped, and
drew blood from my
indolent heart.
If the one-eyed stone would sing,
What could it teach me to be?

10
Dreams

"Dreams are the guiding words of the soul" (Jung)

Five years had passed since I finished making my tapestries and I began to have Holocaust dreams again. I had had Holocaust dreams in the past. They were immobilising, shattering nightmares. The new dreams were patiently instructive with a clear thread running through them. But I was puzzled. I felt that with the completion of the tapestries I had completed my healing task (The One-Eyed Stone, see facing page).

I went into hiding on 17th October. I made 17 tapestries and there were 17 dreams in this series.

The first dream.

The Fairy Tale Healer
I am a therapist and I heal people, especially children. The way I am doing my work is to give the parents a photocopy of a Grimm fairy tale appropriate to their particular child. I do this successfully once. But the second time I lose the relevant tale. I search for it for a very long time. Eventually I find the story in the outside pocket of my travel bag. It is tale no. 41.

I woke up at 3.30 a.m. just like after the operation when I began to draw. The same time of awakening after this dream meant yet again new beginnings, new birth. I wrote the dream down immediately. I knew that it was an important dream. But subsequently I have mislaid it and could not remember its details. I looked for it everywhere with much anxiety. Having to look for the dream mirrored the search in the dream for the lost tale. And just as after a long search I found the tale in the dream, I eventually found the dream in a file called "New Book File". I had completely forgotten that I made such a file and that I had put the dream into it. There was only one other page inside the file. On it I recorded the one sentence I remembered I wrote when I was nine and thought of writing about my war experiences. It said: "the Germans marched into Budapest on the 19th of March 1944". That was all. I don't know why the child in me abandoned the writing. Has she forgotten events or remembered them far too well and decided it is better not to remember and record? I will never know. The file was created to develop the book I wrote after I finished the drawings into a more mature text, but I decided it was not yet the right time. So writing was abandoned again!

What did all this forgetting and remembering, losing and finding mean?

I have repressed most of my memories of hiding, I have lost the "grim tale" which was anything but a cherishable fairy tale but which most of my life I have tried to remember. I believed that the dream was confirming that continuing to search for memories was not what I should be doing. If I were to become my own "wounded healer" I would have to search and find not memories but healing of my woundedness in the grim tale. But how could there possibly be healing hidden in the horrors of that time? I felt the clue must be in the number 41. I did look up the appropriate Grimm fairy tale but it did not really seem relevant. Intuition informed me that this number which arose deep from within myself must point to something more personal in my life. I looked up my drawings of sixteen years ago. Number 41 was "Return". I was astounded.

Unlike at the time of The Last Drawing and Writing (Ch.7), I now realised the immense significance of my image Return (see p.ii). But I thought that I did obey the image. I have returned. I returned to my feelings of profound distress, expressed them through drawings, made meaning of my anguished emotions  with writing, created tapestries to work through those feelings, returned to Budapest and found the house of my hiding, and I reclaimed my birth town.

What was the dream telling me, what more did I have to do? To what did I still have to return?

The dream I had after I returned to Budapest the last time came to mind in which I was allowed to have a glimpse of a new emerging pattern on my kitchen floor. I was intrigued. What will I see? What will the new pattern reveal? Something beneficial I felt, but there was also the intimation in the dream that my inner journey was not over yet; I will still have "to labour and to wait". I was frustrated but also excited and knew I would have to wait for further dreams.

The next dream:

> I had to look for a room in an old house. I end up in a dead end in a dark and forbidding room. I go downstairs and there I find a bright square room. I was told what I had to do.

The dream image is a cul de sac, I cannot go any further and the the place is worn out, old and dark. It seems that what is a fixed structure, a dark room within me has to give away to a new light room. But I could not recall what I had to do and of course ending, allowing the death of something always entails suffering. I braced myself.

> I have to return home from abroad. I am in great danger. A rescue operation is organised by two Jewish people. In the dream a voice was saying " this is a wake-up call, it is the Holocaust."

What the wake-up call was is unmistakable in the next dream:

> Two men turn away from me, saying "We won't talk to you, because you don't have a soul".

The dream imaged the Holocaust as an enormous, horrifying black bug. The strong warning from the two men was, that if I continued to allow this evil bug, my war experience to infest my inner landscape then indeed I would be without a soul, because the space was occupied by the horrors. I was deeply shocked by the dream. It seemed stunningly synchronistic that soon after these two dreams, at a social event, I was told about the existence of Westminster Synagogue which was near my home.

The Holocaust was shown throughout the dreams as a horrifying insect. In time it became more specific and took the shape of a deadly scorpion. It caused terrible agony while at the same time this suffering was denied healing expression. There was a strong emphasis in the dreams to allow the pain to speak. And not merely in spoken words but in written ones. It seemed that writing about my experience of hiding was not only a task but an obligation.

The dreams went on telling me, that although the Holocaust still had the power to haunt and play frightful tricks on me, it was by now a ghost to be put to rest. That if I looked at it with adult eyes I would see that the horrors were de-potentiated. In later dreams the frightful scorpion indeed was shown as a fragile insect like a daddy-long-legs.

The dreams continually instructed me to see and accept this diminishment. It urged me to have the courage to come out of hiding and join the Jewish community. That this would be my final act of healing and I would then become a more complete person.

The last two dreams:

The Black Man

There is a big black man from Africa. His largeness is at the limit of being human. He is very fond of me and visits often. There is something tricky about his written language. A bad statement turns out to be good. He laughs when I discover this. When I kiss him tenderly on his cheek he is delighted. But when he finds out that I am not really in love with him he is devastated. I wake up to his desperately sad sounds as he repeats the words: it is over, it is over, it is over...

This awesome, mercurial big black man laughs when I begin to understand that his message is good. It is as if he is saying: "ah, you thought that I was the blackness of the Holocaust, didn't you? But I am the bringer of good news. I am saying it three times that it is over". He is sad, because I don't quite dare to believe that the Holocaust had loosened its grip, that for me it is over. But he is not giving up on me, he is visiting me often and has high hopes that I will understand and have the courage to trust the needs of my soul. Through the mediation of the transpersonal black man I was asked again not to lose my soul to the dark forces.

The Jewish Place

I am in an open place. There is a lake. There are many, mainly elderly people there. Most of them went through terrible times in 1944 but they had all survived. It is a Jewish place. I am standing somewhat apart from them. A tall, old, good-looking man asks me for a dance. Somewhat reluctantly I accept. I am surprised how pleasant it was, how well we danced together.

In the dream I am returned to an open place where I was not hidden. I am invited to this Jewish place not as a guest, but because I belonged there and I am danced into the community. Dance in my dreams, and also in my waking life, has always been a spiritual experience. The dream was indeed a religious ritual.

Return (Tapestry no.17)

What Can Be Done?

What can be done
when at dawn a black sun awakens
and robs the flowers and grass
of dew and joy and colour?

What can be done
when dark falls where light should have risen,
when plump buds shrivel and die on the stem,
when rivers thirst and dry in their beds?

What can be done
when clouds hang so low over the land
that none but a sprawling mist can be seen
smothering all that breathes and lives and tries to grow?

What can be done is to stand still,
until dawn breaks once more with golden rays
and the rivers are nourished by bursting clouds;
until new shy growth appears on the branches
and the mist, dispersed, shows the Earth
breathing and living and growing again.

What can be done
is to stand still, pregnant with hope.

11
The Return

*"the privilege of a lifetime is to become
who you truly are"* (Jung).

What the dreams repeatedly told me was that return to my Tradition would be my final "return" (interestingly, "dreaming" and "healing" have the same root in Hebrew). Just as I listened to the message of my images I obeyed my dreams and soon after "The Jewish Place" dream I joined Westminster Synagogue.

The Rabbi, Thomas Salamon, was Hungarian and so amazingly my Jewish and Hungarian roots instantly met and interlinked. At our first meeting I told him my story, and then said with a measure of discomfort that I didn't know what to do. He replied and I quote: " You don't have to do anything. You are a Jew. Do whatever is comfortable." Instantly I felt a sense of relief and acceptance.

When I attended my first ever religious service and the Torah was taken out and carried around I was deeply stirred. Finally, I was partaking in a ritual that had been performed for two thousand years. When the Torah passed by me I instinctively touched it with my fingers. My eyes were wet with tears. I was utterly taken aback by these involuntary reactions and emotions.

The sermon was about Moses. And it came to me that the story of Moses is my story also. I too was cast away as a child on to the dark waters of uncertainty and I too was rescued.

I realised I was not a hidden child I was a saved one!

I knew that I had much work ahead of me. Much had been lost, but by some small miracle my grandmother's candlestick holders, which my mother used to light on Friday nights, survived. When I was young I did not know about Friday nights. Religion was not allowed during the communist era and I thought the candle lighting in the corner of a room was my mother's private ritual.

Now I began to light them on Friday nights. I learned the blessings and observed the Sabbath. I went to services and attended all the festivals. I began to read the Torah and everything to do with Judaism. I thirsted and hungered for all that revealed the wisdom, the beauty, the rituals and the mystery of this ancient Tradition. And as I studied and observed, instead of terror and shame I became proud of this ancient treasure which was always mine but which I never knew I had.

It was deeply satisfying whenever I found a Biblical event or theme which found an echo in my own life. I read in a book on Genesis that Joseph named his first son Manasseh. He has named him for forgetfulness. In him Joseph was celebrating the oblivion of his trials. He was grateful that God made him forget his hardship. I realised again that forgetting much of my wartime trauma was a blessing rather than a loss I needed to atone for.

The night before my first Yom Kippur, the most sacred festival in the Jewish calendar, I had a dream which I called the 18th. It reminded me of my image The Dragon Babies (see following page) and the poem "Vision" which I wrote about it a few years ago. The dream chronicled my painstaking endeavours and made it clear that I was now ready to embark on the last stage of my healing journey. I began to learn Hebrew and decided to do the right of passage of a Bat Mitzvah.

Bar/Bat Mitzvahs are unique, solemn and moving occasions. They are individual but also collective events where a person declares his or her faith and makes a solemn promise to lead a Jewish life.

It was on the 17th October in 1944 that I went into hiding and I decided that it will be on the same date, on the 17th October sixty-five years later to the day that I would do my Bat Mitzvah. Preparing for it was emotionally hard, intense and trying. At one point the date I chose made me anxious and I had

The Dragon Babies (Tapestry no.15)

Vision

I saw a serpent in the night,
it swished and coiled and
bit its tail, and gave birth
to a thousand stars.
And in a sky so strangely
lit, I saw the world
in a circle swirl, and
a crowd on mighty scales.
And my unsung words
had tipped those scales,
and my deeds were
reflected in the stars.

time with Rabbi Thomas to talk things over. He made me fully aware of how wholly different the events of those two dates really were. My Bat Mitzvah was to be the direct opposite of my war experience. It would be light not dark. I did not need to hide for fear of death, I could stand up without fear and declare my faith.

Perhaps to compensate for my temporary emotional turbulence, learning Hebrew was surprisingly easy. When sometimes it was difficult I said to myself it is better to wake up with incomprehensible Hebrew words in my mouth than with Holocaust nightmares. Early on I came across a quote which said that "for the displaced and dislocated, for those uprooted century after century, language remains the constant, the place where safety resides." I felt this keenly. After Rabbi Thomas taught me the alphabet I decided to study on my own. Learning the prayers and the parashah, the portion of the Torah I was required to read, was a joyful time. I looked forward to it each day. I have a sense since, that there must exist something like a collective memory. It must be that the ancient sounds, repeated century after century get transmitted through time and space, and I have heard and recognised them.

I bought myself a beautiful golden necklace of the Star of David to wear for the occasion. The discriminatory badge of shame thus became a joyful declaration. It was like a song in my heart silencing the sounds of black boots echoing in my soul in the dark of night.

During the time of studying a supportive network was woven around me. Friends, family, people from the synagogue and others sent messages, shared experiences, well-wishing me to succeed. This was extraordinary and utterly unexpected. Sixty-five years ago people were after me, now they were for me. No words can describe the difference.

I kept in touch with my analyst as a friend and colleague. He came to my Bat Mitzvah and contributed by reading my favourite psalm from the bimah.

Usually only men wear the tallit (prayer shawl) and the yarmulka (skull cap). I asked Rabbi Thomas would he mind if I wore them and he said he would, but that I must do what felt right for me. So contrary to tradition I wore both a tallit and a yarmulka while reading from the Torah. It helped me feel the presence of the Shekinah, the female presence of God and gave a special feminine holiness and transcendence to my Day.

That my portion, synchronistically, was the very first words of Genesis B'reshit, the Beginning, the creation of the world, the greatest mystery of all, was awesome. The earth was without form and void "*Tohu va vohu*" and God created order out of chaos. This imaginative creative ordering found an echo in my own life. My return to Judaism on one level was about ordering my past chaotic experiences. My Bat Mitzvah was a celebration of that order.

The Torah scroll from which I read my parashah was a Czech scroll. Over 1500 scrolls came to Westminster Synagogue from Prague, where they were gathered from synagogues destroyed by the Nazis. They were rescued and restored and most of them have been sent out to Jewish communities all over the world. It was my privilege to read my portion from one of these Czech scrolls which was retained by my synagogue. I felt deeply moved and privileged to read from it. I too felt rescued and restored. I felt the triumph of continuation, of survival, my own and that of my people. An affirmation that the Torah cannot be destroyed. And nor can the People of the Book be destroyed.

I was called up to read from the Torah by my chosen Jewish name Miriam. As I did not know my parents' Jewish names Rabbi Thomas suggested that I was called up as the daughter of Avraham and Sarah. The continued relevance and aptness of going back to the beginning touched me deeply.

Though I was throughout the Celebration in a different dimension altogether, on another level I felt the tremendous energy in the Sanctuary, everyone feeling with me, willing me, supporting and helping me through it all. It was a kind of birth, the congregation the midwife. If archetypally the Holocaust was my death, my rebirth was my return to my Tradition. It was the end of spiritual death and the beginning of confidence and joy of who I was.

My parashah was about beginning and creativity and so was my return to the Tradition, signalling a new beginning in my life as a Jew. My Bat Mitzvah was a creative affirmation and completion of my identity. I listened to my dreams. I returned and rescued the hidden child. I brought her out into the open, out of the darkness to the light by returning to myself that part of herself which has remained hidden for over six decades: her Jewish identity. I was hidden no longer. My long and painstaking journey of two decades was finally over. By some divine energy I had been returned to my people, my tradition, my full identity. I felt and feel healed and whole.

I made a tapestry for my Bat Mitzvah, the eighteenth, ten years after completing the others, echoing my eighteenth dream. I called it The Bridge. It contains all my experiences, my wounding as well as my healing. Horror as well as redemption, joy as well as sorrow, mourning as well as recovery are threaded through it. Despite the fear, despite the terrible knowledge about evil which I had carried in my heart since a child, I now lived a full life. This is my triumphant and creative response to the dark forces. And this is the meaning of all my images. That creativity, not bitterness and hate, is the answer, the redemptive force.

The Bridge

The Bridge (Tapestry no.18)

Afterword

I discovered that text and textile have the same Latin root "texere", meaning to weave. A linear thread runs through both the written page and a tapestry. At the exhibition of the tapestries I said I hoped that at a future date my words and my images, text and textile would be woven together, giving my experience a more complete form.

The first time I attempted to write about 1944 was right after the war when I was still nine years old. It was abandoned. The second time was after I finished drawing, but though the writing was a courageous attempt it was unprocessed and raw. The third time was when I returned to my Tradition. I wanted to obey that particular dream in the series of seventeen, which said that writing about the Holocaust was not just a task but an obligation. However I felt that for the writing to be complete I had to experience and live a Jewish life for awhile.

This is then the fourth time and I now feel that I fulfilled the obligation the dream was talking about. I understood that the obligation was to write about the effects of the Holocaust and also about the possibility of healing. And that healing comes about through finding meaning and through creativity. And importantly it is an obligation because as a hidden child I am one of the last witnesses. When we all die, the facts hopefully will remain undistorted. But the survivors' anguished witnessing and recollections will die with them. I feel that having written my story the best I could, I finally fulfilled my obligation to my inner world and also to the outer one.

I made one more tapestry. I called it Loss. (See facing page.) But I could have called it "radical acceptance" or even tranquillity…

Loss

Loss (Tapestry no.19 from Drawing no.33)

Though I, and probably others, might have been able to haul ourselves out of the Holocaust by creating a meaningful narrative for ourselves or by some other individual means, the Holocaust remains the unspeakable monstrosity it was and is. Is, because it is still an open wound, mourned by the first generation of survivors, is affecting the second, and sadly also the third. Comments, lacking in imagination such as "let it go, it happened decades ago", open the wound just that bit wider. This historical traumatic wounding will never be forgotten. It will be forever remembered.

As someone observed, we must remind ourselves that the Holocaust was not six million. It was one, plus one plus one...Each victim murdered was an individual, a unique irreplaceable human being.

"People are accustomed to look at the heavens and wonder what happened there. It would be better if they would (also) look within themselves to see what happens there." (Rabbi Menachem Mendel of Kotsk).

The Images

Do you live life strictly by
calendar dates? Do you measure
love daily on lukewarm scales?
Do you work with devotion
on charting the colours
of butterfly wings? And
do you, like beavers, dam up
the rivers, and build fences to
limit your world?

Dare you travel with the
'bride of the wind'? Above the
forest of night she gallops on
her strange horse freely.
Look, how her soft shape
alters, as she dances to the
groaning music of trees.
Keenly the black-eyed sun
looks up from the forest floor.
The branch twists and turns,
jailer to the spirit of the bird.

No sense in these
broken images you say?
Yet they make nonsense
of your sunlit walk
through everydays.

Look closely, look into
this mirror shattered, and
see infinity beckoning
in each fragmented shape.

Marika Henriques

The Drawings

First Steps (Drawing no.1)

The Bed of Pain (Drawing no.2)

The Queen Bee (Drawing no.3)

Therapy (Drawing no.4)

My Tree of Life (Drawing no.5)

The Jewel
(Drawing no.6)

The Jewel (Drawing no.7)

Survival (Drawing no.8)

Flowers (Drawing no.9)

Flowers (Drawing no.10)

Flowers (Drawing no.11)

Distress (Drawing no.12)

Protrusion (Drawing no.13)

The Snake (Drawing no.14)

The Figurine (Drawing no.15)

Deflation (Drawing no.16)

Mysterious
Couples
(Drawing no.17)

Mysterious
Couples
(Drawing no.18)

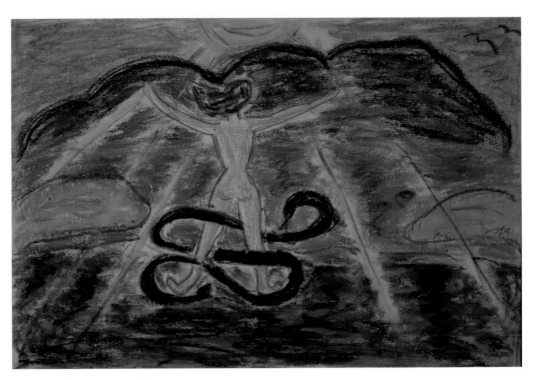

Conquest (Drawing no.19)

The Chaos Dragon (Drawing no.20)

The Spiral Snake (Drawing no.21)

Night Terrors (Drawing no.22)

The Obliterated Child (Drawing no.23)

From Clear Skies (Drawing no.24)

The Joke (Drawing no.25)

The Two Little Mourners (Drawing no.26)

The Mute One
(Drawing no.27)

Ambivalent Pregnancy (Drawing no.28)

The Forest (Drawing no.29)

The Desert (Drawing no.30)

The Four Sisters (Drawing no.31)

Defeat (Drawing no.32)

Dying (Drawing no.33)

The Egg (Drawing no.34)

The Well of Tears (Drawing no.35)

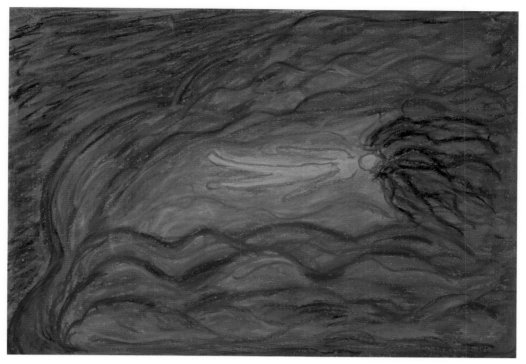

Respite (Drawing no.36)

The Sky Father (Drawing no.37)

Heart Container (Drawing no.38)

Arrows (Drawing no.39)

Arrows (Drawing no.40)

Return (Drawing no.41)

Heart Flower (Drawing no.42)

Bird and Snake (Drawing no.43)

Portrait of my Analyst (Drawing no.44)

Laying a Ghost (Drawing no.45)

Forsaken (Drawing no.46)

The Snake Girl (Drawing no.47)

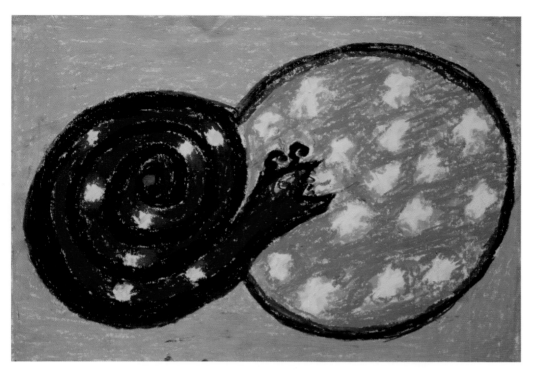

The Dragon Babies (Drawing no.48)

The One-Eyed Stone (Drawing no.49)

The Dancer
(Drawing no.50)

The Acid Bath Murderer (Drawing no.51)

Death (Drawing no.52)

The Tapestries

The tapestries are displayed in the order in which they were stitched.

The Snake Girl (Tapestry no.14)

The Dragon Babies (Tapestry no.15)

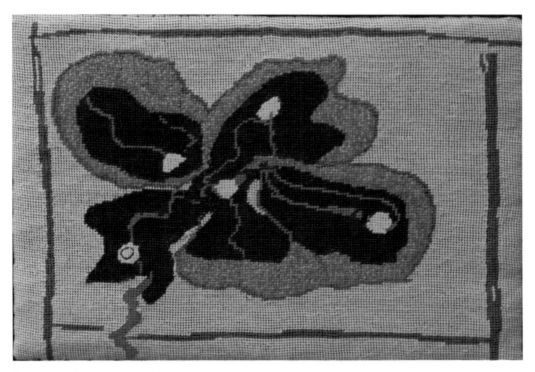

Protrusion (Tapestry no.16)

Night Terrors (Tapestry no.11)

Bird and Snake (Tapestry no.4)

The Forest (Tapestry no.6)

The Mute One
(Tapestry no.2)

Death (Tapestry no.8)

The Two Little Mourners (Tapestry no.12)

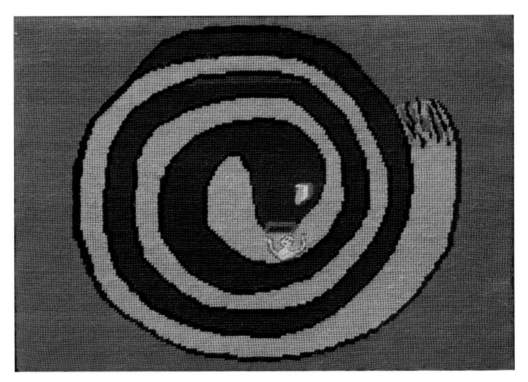

The Spiral Snake (Tapestry no.3)

Return (Tapestry no.17)

The Sky Father (Tapestry no.13)

The One-Eyed Stone (Tapestry no.7))

The Acid Bath Murderer (ABM) (Tapestry no.1)

Forsaken (Tapestry no.10)

The Snake Girl (Tapestry no.5)

The Dancer
(Tapestry no.9)

The Bridge (Tapestry no.18)

Loss (Tapestry no.19)